Karate

RULES

Karate
RULES

BRYAN EVANS

WARD LOCK

A WARD LOCK BOOK
First published in the UK 1998
by Ward Lock
Wellington House
125 Strand
LONDON
WC2R 0BB

A Cassell Imprint

Distributed in the United States
by Sterling Publishing Co., Inc.
387 Park Avenue South, New York,
NY 10016–8810

A British Library Cataloguing in Publication Data
block for this book may be obtained from the
British Library

ISBN 0-7063-7669-2

Design and computer page make up by
Penny Mills
Printed and bound in Great Britain by
The Bath Press,

1095

CONTENTS

The legendary Terry
O'Neill (left), now a
successful television
and movie actor,
looking to dispatch
another opponent in a
National
Championship.
O'Neill was a
flamboyant, exciting
fighter, who
mesmerized audiences
with his inventive and
effective fighting style.

CONVERSION TABLE

1 millimetre (mm) = 0.03 inch
1 centimetre (cm) = 0.93 inch
1 metre (m)   = 1.09 yards, 3.28 feet
1 kilometre (km)   = 0.62 mile
1 gram (g)   = 0.03 ounce
1 kilogram (kg)   = 2.20 pounds, 0.15 stone
1 millilitre (ml) = 0.03 fluid ounce

Temperature conversion

$$°C = (°F - 32) \times 5$$

INTRODUCTION

This book aims to provide the *karateka* (karate practitioner) with all the information necessary in order to enter competitions. It is not a work intended for the referee or the judge; rather it is simply a handbook of rules for the 'player' so that, having read it, he may be better informed, able to perform within the rules and become a more successful competitor. Yet it has to be said that reading a book alone cannot guarantee success – only hard work in the *dojo* (karate hall), practising *kata* (techniques) relentlessly and facing high-calibre opponents can do that. But an inexperienced *karateka*, even one who is highly skilled, would be very lucky indeed to make it through to the finals with little or no knowledge of the rules. Furthermore, there is some merit to the notion that knowing the rules can in many circumstances be used to one's own advantage.

These factors alone should provide enough incentive for regarding the learning of these rules as an integral part of every competitor's championship preparation.

Knowing the rules governing both the *kumite* (sparring) and *kata* events will enable the *karateka* to appreciate how and why decisions are made. This book should therefore prove useful as a guide for both the novice competitor and the more experienced *karateka* who simply wishes to brush up on his knowledge. It will also be invaluable for the enthusiastic, but often bewildered, spectator, who until now has been perplexed by the judges' incomprehensible signals. The book also includes sections dealing with the criteria used by the referee for awarding points in *kumite* and an insight into how *kata* performance is judged.

NOTE

Throughout this book the terms 'he' and 'his' have been used for convenience, and should be taken to include women as well as men.

1 EVOLUTION OF SPORT KARATE

The deadly martial arts of eastern Asia flourished as a direct consequence of centuries of continual unrest between neighbouring cultures. This volatile milieu frequently erupted into all-out war in an age long before enthusiastic audiences would applaud combat skills displayed for mere entertainment. In Japan, in particular, there was a proliferation of the methods involving the use of weapons, which became known as the 'classical' martial arts, or *bu-jitsu*. Not surprisingly, weaponless combat throughout the Middle Ages almost fell into disuse, because an unarmed man, even possessing great expertise, had little chance against the martial skills of an armed, fully armoured warrior. The emphasis throughout this period was definitely on the aquisition of skills primarily concerned with the effective usage of weapons, especially the sword.

It was not until about the mid-sixteenth century, during periods of relative peace, that the classical martial arts were gradually replaced by unarmed combat systems. This was no accident, as the transformation from *bu-jitsu* to weaponless fighting was actively encouraged by Shoguns (military dictators) who had a vested interest in ensuring that control was maintained over those they ruled. Of course, the simple act of banning weapons inevitably provided the springboard for the development of unarmed combat, but it appears that this was tolerated, possibly because such arts were comparatively less efficient from a military standpoint.

Furthermore, there was a discernible shift from the purely martial or military application of combat towards more ethical concepts such as self-enlightenment and the perfection of the character. *Bu-jitsu* therefore gave way to *bu-do*, or 'martial ways'. In many ways, however, this was a façade. We know today that deception played a large part in the evolution of the martial arts – the truth being that exponents were not only secretly developing lethal unarmed combat methods but also modifying everyday tools and farming implements into weapons that were intended for anything but perfecting the character!

Karate, as practised today, is considered a modern martial art, although it was derived from earlier unarmed combat systems generally referred to as *ju-jutsu*. Those earlier arts, unlike modern karate, were largely devoid of any ethical code, their sole purpose being their efficiency in the destruction of the enemy. However, like the classical martial arts, karate quickly became an effective and proven method of self-defence. *Karate-do*, literally 'empty-hand-way', underwent many refinements as it was developed. Techniques were examined scientifically in order to improve mechanical efficiency and to promote health, so that karate became more than just a system of self-defence. It was infused with a moral code of conduct, an attribute that would have been unsuited on the battlefield where survival was the name of the game. With the need for self-protection on the decline, however, the more philosophical aspects of the martial arts gained eminence.

Nevertheless, fighting spirit proved to be irrepressible, heralded by the intense rivalry between differing *ryu* or schools. Any 'contests' that did take place were conducted in deadly seriousness and often served to settle disputes. Stories abound of one school of martial arts, or one 'champion', challenging another to determine who was superior, with the result that deaths were commonplace. On the island of Okinawa, where modern karate originated, there was never any real attempt to introduce rules that would allow participants to test their skills safely. Any suggestion of 'watering down' the art by removing the more dangerous elements for the sake of sport was met with fierce opposition. For the Okinawans, karate was first and foremost a martial art.

Only when karate was introduced to the Japanese mainland in 1922 was there a serious attempt to introduce rules to permit the free exchange of techniques during sparring. Many masters of the time strongly resisted this move, some maintaining that, as karate was a defensive art and a method of developing the character, there could be no justification for indulging in a practice that actively encouraged combatants to attack one another. With the growing popularity of karate, however, it became clear that Okinawan tradition alone would not prevent karate from developing as a sport

as well. Once adopted by the Japanese, karate was absorbed into its culture and subjected to many subtle changes. Initially, pre-arranged sparring was introduced, as this was considered safer. Participants would assume the role of attacker or defender, therefore ensuring that the practice of karate could be justified morally – something that was perhaps more acceptable as far as the 'traditionalists' were concerned.

Jyu-kumite, or freestyle fighting, in spite of great opposition, became ever more popular with the young *karateka* who were eager to test their skills against those who were similarly trained. Rules to prohibit certain dangerous techniques were introduced, but in the early days it seems that there was little effort to control such techniques; clashes often degenerated into full-contact bouts, resulting in appalling injuries and even death. This practice was quite understandably shunned by the leading masters of the time, who sought a compromise and so began discussions to formalize an agreed set of rules. The aim was to ensure that fighters could test the effectiveness of their art and yet place their 'opponents' beyond danger.

The practitioners of the many divergent styles of karate were generally in agreement about what practices were considered safe or unsafe. For example, open-hand strikes utilizing the fingertips aimed at vital points were banned, as were kicks to joints and any throwing techniques or locks that were considered too dangerous. The practice of striking at the opponent with full power was condemned, and the concept of *sun-dome* or control was formulated. This essentially meant that combatants could still throw their techniques with full force, but all blows had to be focused just short of skin contact. It is perhaps interesting that

Veteran competitor Jimmy Brennan, now retired, launches a long *gyaku-zuki* attack which just misses the target during a team match at a National Championship.

the modern concept of control permits *karateka* to make contact, with the condition that there are degrees of control: blows can be delivered with palpable impact to the body, whereas contact to the head and face must be limited to skin contact. The generally accepted term to describe this method is 'controlled contact' and this, in the author's opinion, should replace the ambiguous term 'semi-contact', which is in fact a misnomer.

In 1964 an officially recognized governing body, the Federation of All Japan Karate-do Organizations (FAJKO), united the many different styles of karate in Japan under the first agreed rules for competition karate, and the stage was set for modern sport karate. In 1969, the first All Japan

Karate Championship was held under FAJKO rules. Since that time karate has become truly international, but unfortunately has also suffered huge political problems, causing modern karate to be fragmented into several world governing bodies. However, most are agreed on the principles as set out by FAJKO, and it is these rules and regulations that persist today in one form or another, although as karate competition has continued to improve, the need for rules to be updated and improved has been recognized, and they are constantly under review. (As a footnote, this brief history of sport karate concerns the development of 'traditional' competitive karate – sport as a derivative of the recognized oriental fighting arts – and not the full-contact 'karate' or kick-boxing, which is an American invention.)

2 TYPES OF KARATE COMPETITION

Skill in karate is expressed in competition by two separate but related disciplines. *Karateka* can demonstrate their mastery of technique, strategy and tactics by entering the *kumite* or free sparring event. This category consists of an individual event and also a team event. Competitors will endeavour to secure victory by defeating an opponent using the free exchange of legal and controlled techniques. The other form of competition, *kata*, enables the *karateka* to demonstrate, without the use of an opponent, mastery of form and technical skills by performing a set routine of defensive and attacking techniques. As with the *kumite* event, this category also enables competitors to enter on an individual basis and again as a member of a team.

Competitors are grouped by age and gender in all the *kumite* events, although there is now the opportunity for both male and females to compete in the team *kata* events. Victory or defeat is decided in both *kata* and *kumite* events by a team of qualified judges who will base their decision on the criteria established in the rules. An arbitrator is appointed to ensure the fairness of the conduct of the matches and that all judgements are made in accordance with the agreed procedures. In addition, to ensure the smooth running of events, a time-keeper, a record-keeper and an announcer are appointed. A brief introduction to the various forms of competition follows below.

KUMITE COMPETITION

The individual event

In keeping with all forms of competition, competitors in the individual *kumite* event have to survive elimination rounds in order to progress to the finals. For the elimination rounds, all the entries are pooled and a list is produced pairing all the competitors. As each pair is called up, one of the two competitors is instructed to tie a red belt around his own belt for identification purposes. Thus he is designated the 'red' competitor, or *aka*. His opponent is referred to as *shiro*, the 'white' competitor, although it is not usual for him actually to wear a white belt.

Matches in the elimination rounds are usually conducted using the two-man system, sometimes referred to as the 'mirror' system. This involves the use of a chief referee supported by an assistant referee, and is described in detail on p. 46. The competitors are instructed to fight, with the winner being declared by the chief referee. The successful competitor then progresses to the next round, and so on until he is beaten or survives to qualify

Ex-international Bob Rhodes referees the female individual *kumite* at the 1997 National Championship. The fighter to the right, Julie Nicholson, is 12 times *kata* champion. Her competition ambition is to become the KUGB's first female grand champion, gaining first place in both *kata* and *kumite*.

for the 'finals'. These consist of the quarter-finals (the last eight), the semi-finals (the last four) and ultimately the final itself.

Competitors who have been successful in previous championships, achieving a position as high as perhaps the last four, may, in accordance with the championship rules, be seeded through to the quarter-finals; this means that they will meet the best competitors from the day's eliminations. One advantage of this system is that it benefits the less experienced competitor who otherwise, despite having fought admirably through the opening round, may then meet an established champion in the very next round. Such a confrontation, if permitted so early in the championship, would probably shake the confidence of the most determined hopeful! By removing elite performers from the elimination rounds, other competitors have the opportunity to progress further, and thereby gain valuable experience.

Another consideration, perhaps more from the spectators' viewpoint, is that the seeding system practically ensures that only quality competitors make it to the finals. No spectator, having purchased a ticket, wants to watch competitors who are obviously not 'up to the mark' fighting for the top honours.

The quarter-finals, semi-finals and final are usually conducted using a single chief referee and four corner judges. The chief referee has absolute authority over the match, but he is required in certain situations to obtain the advice of the four corner judges. The corner judges signal their opinions to the referee by using a flag system. Each judge holds a red flag, which refers to *aka*, in one hand, and a white flag, which refers to *shiro*, in the other.

The team event

A team generally comprises five members with one reserve, although international matches, owing to the high cost of sending delegates abroad, are sometimes fought with just three members. A team, in principle, should comprise an odd number, plus one reserve. As briefly described above, matches are conducted on an individual basis, using the system of one referee and four corner judges, in a predetermined order, with the team accumulating the most wins achieving victory. If there is a draw, the referee will decide the winning team based upon the criteria described on p. 48. Should a decision still prove to be elusive, a single representative from each team will be required to fight to obtain a result.

Opposing competitors are identified in the same way as for the individual event.

Ippon kumite event

This is a new event adopted by the Karate Union of Great Britain (KUGB), and in many ways combines the qualities necessary for the good performance for both *kata* and *kumite*. Competitors are paired, each being identified in the usual way. They take it in turns to attack and defend nominated targets in a predetermined manner, using selected and stated techniques. The winning competitor, having demonstrated good form and superior skill and attitude, is announced by the referee and progresses to the next round.

KATA COMPETITION

The individual event

The performance of *kata* in competition allows the *karateka* the opportunity to demonstrate technical excellence and the spirit of *bu-do* (martial ways). *Shotokan kata* has evolved to become a visually beautiful expression of the art, and competitors will need to demonstrate spirit, control over form, breathing and focus. The individual *kata* event is composed of the elimination rounds and the finals. As with the *kumite* event, all entries are pooled and the competitors are paired. The prescribed *kata* for the eliminations in KUGB events are normally the *heian kata* 1–5. As each pair is called up, one competitor is designated *aka* and the other *shiro* as in the *kumite* event. Both are required to perform a *kata* simultaneously, selected at random from a list by the chief judge. A direct comparison is then made by the judges and a decision is made, the winner being announced by the chief judge. The winner then goes into the next round to compete in the same way. This continues until the number of competitors is reduced to usually eight or four, depending on the initial number of competitors.

The judges (usually five, including the chief judge) are positioned around the perimeter of the area. The chief judge sits at the front, directly facing the competitors, and (as in the *kumite* event) the remainder sit at the corners. The flag system is used to decide the winner, with a different system for the finals (explained below). The judges each carry a red flag (for *aka*) and a white flag (for *shiro*). The chief judge makes all the commands, and blows a whistle to obtain results from the other judges. They indicate their preference simultaneously by raising the appropriate flag and, taking his own opinion into account, the chief judge declares the winner by flag signal. In the event of a draw, the contestants are required to perform further *kata* selected from the list, until a result is obtained.

For the finals, as previously mentioned, another method of judging is normally used. This involves a 'points' system in which the judges, usually seven including the chief judge, raise numbered cards indicating a score. These scores are combined, with the lowest and highest mark being disregarded, to determine the final score. The competitor scoring the highest marks is declared the winner. Competitors are asked to perform their favourite *kata*, which should include those relative to their *kyu* or Dan level. For the brown- and black-belt categories, it is usual for the contestants to be required to perform a *kata* other than those of the elimination rounds.

The team event

A team comprises three members (all male, all female, or a mixture). The elimination rounds and finals are usually conducted using the points system of judging in the same way as the final of the individual event. An extra challenge inherent in this category is that of precise timing. Despite accomplished individual performances within the team, it is vitally important that all members of the team are perfectly synchronized, otherwise the overall effect is untidy and points are deducted. In this category, it is usual, even in the elimination rounds, for each team to perform a *kata* of their choice. However, as with the individual event, should a team progress to the finals, a different *kata* must be selected. The usual procedure of tying a red belt around the waist for identification purposes does not apply in this event.

OPPOSITE Frank Brennan, perhaps the most successful competitor ever, shows his extraordinary ability to a captivated audience during a National Championship. Here, demonstrating concentration and masterful form, he is midway through another winning performance of the advanced *kata* called *niju-shiho*.

3 THE MATCH AREA

The rules dictate that, for the purposes of *kumite*, the match area should be a flat, unobstructed surface measuring 8m². The boundary of the area is clearly marked and two parallel lines, each 1m long, placed 3m apart, are positioned near the centre to indicate the standing positions of the competitors. That is just about all that is required, although there is mention in the rules of the need to take 'necessary measures' to prevent accidents. What this amounts to is that the flooring should be suitable in order to minimize the possibility of injury, particularly as competitors are at risk from falls as a result of *ashi-barai* or leg-sweeps. Although the risk of injury from falls is not considered to be as great as would be expected during a judo match, a sprung wooden floor, provided it is not highly polished, is generally considered the acceptable surface and provides enough 'give' in the event of a tumble. In addition, this type of flooring is what one would normally expect to find in the traditional *dojo*, and therefore has the advantage of feeling familiar under foot. The match area itself should be situated well away from any obstructions, and should incorporate a 'safety area' surrounding it and extending 1m beyond its boundaries.

It is increasingly commonplace to see karate and judo using matting similar to that used in gymnastic displays. This 'modern' safety flooring is ideal in that it provides a very firm and yet yielding surface to ensure that where there is accidental impact against the floor, particularly involving the head, the risk of serious injury is reduced. There have been incidents in the past where competitors have been knocked unconscious, not as might be expected from the result of a blow, but because the unfortunate player's head has struck a solid floor. Even accepting that excessive contact may have been instrumental in such cases, it is obvious just how important the suitability of the floor area is in our sport. I am sure that judo players, or even gymnasts, would suffer grave doubts if they were faced with the prospect of performing without the 'safety net' of high-quality matting. As competitors in pursuit of greater excellence risk more injury, there is quite rightly an ever-increasing emphasis being placed on safety issues.

4 EQUIPMENT AND SAFETY

The only 'equipment' needed to compete is your *karate-gi* (uniform), which should be clean, white and unmarked save for a club or association badge. Sleeves should not be rolled up during *kumite* as this practice can result in injury to an opponent's fingers or toes as a consequence of becoming ensnared. Some judges also instruct *kata* competitors to roll down their sleeves, although this would seem to be somewhat unnecessary given that there is no opponent to injure.

Most personal protective devices are not allowed in World Shotokan Karate Association (WSKA) events. Exceptions are the compulsory gumshield and groin guards (highly recommended for men) and breast protectors (highly recommended for women). An accidental kick or low punch that strikes the groin could result in the loss of a testicle, and receiving a heavy punch to delicate breast tissue is not recommended. Headguards, shin and instep protectors and sparring mitts, however, are illegal. This is because it is expected that competitors are able to exhibit the highest degree of control (see below) and, accidents aside, demonstrate this skill by controlling the amount of force in any offensive or defensive technique. This makes the need for ostentatious protection unnecessary.

If you wish to enter a competition wearing a bandage to protect an injury sustained previously, you should always seek the advice of the chief judge and medical officer on the day. It may be that the bandage will be regarded as a potential risk or that your injury compels the medical officer to declare you unfit to compete. In any event, it is always better to attend to these details before being called up to compete in order to save time and avoid inconvenience.

Good standards of hygiene should be observed, and fingernails and toenails should be kept clean and short. In keeping with *dojo* etiquette, the wearing of jewellery, rings and watches is forbidden. Any rings that cannot be removed should be covered with tape to prevent injury.

SAFETY THROUGH CONTROL

Control of technique is paramount, so that competitors win, not with a show of brute force or the dubious and certainly unhealthy 'ability' to take punishment, but with the demonstration of superior skill over an opponent who is similarly trained.

Control is related to distancing. As novices, we are instructed to extend our techniques fully; indeed there is an emphasis placed on thrusting techniques as opposed to those involving a snapping action. This is to enable the novice to lock out his limbs when delivering kicks and punches, thereby completing techniques, or fully extending them. In forcefully and completely extending a limb, it is essential that muscular contraction at the point of near-full extension brings about a halt to an action that would otherwise damage joints and tendons. The body will naturally 'apply the brakes' in order to prevent self-injury, and it is this automatic physiological response that is utilized and developed to produce *kime* (the focus of power). The *karateka* learns to apply this phenomenon to the entire body so that the resulting instantaneous muscular contraction releases and transmits enormous energy to the intended target.

A problem arises, however, when karate technique is applied to the contest situation, where an opponent is involved. If there is a predominance of thrusting techniques, so that arms and legs are almost fully locked out, distancing would have to be pretty much constant in every situation. Of course it never is. This makes the use of such techniques very limited, and in some cases downright dangerous. To emphasize this point, consider punching at your opponent's face using a thrusting *kizami-zuki* (jab punch). This would be appropriate in a basic sparring routine, where your opponent is stationary, the distance is fixed and your attacking arm is held fully extended, fist just touching the target. Try translating this to a free sparring situation, however, where the circumstances are completely different, and the result could be very hazardous for your opponent. For a start, the distance is never fixed because you

will both be manoeuvering for an advantage. For this reason, you can never be absolutely sure of where the target will be once you have launched your attack. Should your opponent rush at you as you release your thrusting punch, the committed nature of your attack would effectively spear him as his face tries to occupy the same space as your fist!

This is precisely why snapping techniques are primarily used in free fighting. The action of snapping, or sharply pulling back, is a technique perfectly suited to a situation where distance cannot be guaranteed. The advantage of the snapping action lies in its suitability to be used over any range, so that a *karateka* can punch effectively at very close range without having to extend the arm fully, as in the thrust version. Being able to snap a technique back is considered to be an advanced way of delivering kicks, punches and strikes, and this is reflected in the grading syllabus where novices are required to demonstrate predominantly thrust techniques. This is perhaps why we see more injuries in *kyu* grade sparring. It could be that they have yet to be able to exploit the snapping technique fully, being bound habitually by the need to lock out or complete their strikes whatever the distance.

I remember a very interesting and exhilarating training session I had some years ago with *sensei* (instructor) Bob Poynton, in which he had the class practise a fast snapping *gyaku-zuki* (reverse punch) against a partner repeatedly rushing in. Each time the opponent

OPPOSITE World Championships, Sunderland 1990. A Japanese competitor leaps in with what appears to be a threatened low *mawashi-geri* – actually a ruse to draw his opponent's guard down in order to create an opening for a possible follow-up *jodan* punch.

would start from a distance just out of reach, launching forward suddenly with the intention of closing the gap as quickly as possible. The defender was instructed by Poynton to snap out his punch accurately and precisely at fractionally different times so that sometimes the opponent would be caught at the full extent of reach, and at other times at very close distance. Whatever the range, it was vital, particularly as the target was the opponent's chin, to stop the punch and snap it back every time with only the slightest of touches. Punching in this way exemplifies the best form needed for competition, where it is not necessary or recommended to lock out a punching arm fully.

The above exercise, simple though it was, really brought home the importance of good control, and that it is not something that necessarily comes with general training. The conclusion is that one needs to approach training in a very specific way, by using drills that are specially designed to develop and maintain the ability to control fast snapping techniques. If all competitors trained in this way instead of allowing, as some do, their opponent's body to stop their technique, the match area would be a safer place. Unfortunately, there is still a great deal of machismo associated with entering *kumite* events, and it is thought by many that injuries come with the territory. This attitude is acceptable up to a point, but it must be remembered that karate is for everyone, and that participating in a *kumite* event should not be viewed as being exclusively for 'roughnecks', or a way of giving or receiving a 'good hiding'.

Disputes over the appropriateness of protective wear continue, although it must be said that those who recommend, indeed seek to justify, the use of such equipment are usually unqualified to uphold any claims regarding safety issues. They would seem to be unaware of, or choose to ignore, the hidden dangers. Investigation into claims that the wearing of protection prevents more serious injury from occurring has revealed without question that there is a distinct lack of control where such devices are authorized. In effect, it provides those who have little regard for their opponent's safety with a licence to hit harder. Medical and scientific opinion overwhelmingly supports the view of many 'traditionalists' that providing fighters with hand and foot protection exchanges otherwise relatively innocuous facial injuries for the far more serious consequences of blunt head injury.

More worrying still is the mounting concern that suggests that even children, let alone adults, who are allowed to compete wearing protectors may hit with sufficient force to cause concussive injuries. Contentious though it may be, we only have to look to the boxing ring to establish the long-term effects of repeated blunt head injury. Without doubt, despite the 'protection' of boxing gloves, trauma of this kind is cumulative and, significantly, usually only becomes apparent in later life. The several highly publicized boxing fatalities of recent years would suggest that such trauma may also be hastened by a single, yet deadly, blow. In the martial arts, the problem with mitt protectors and the like is that, in allowing competitors to wear such equipment, there is evidence that control is subsequently relaxed in the mistaken belief that the light padding provided will have a cushioning effect, thereby reducing injury. As discussed, this is patently not true. On the other hand, without such devices the competitor becomes acutely aware of the possibility of self-injury and of his potential to damage his opponent, and that the slightest misjudgment can result in injury and disqualification. This, therefore, can only be a positive thing, as competition in which a high degree of skill and control is required will encourage the best technique, while actively discouraging those with less ability who would otherwise enter having little regard for control or excellence of technique.

As an antidote to the belief that only full force is exciting, I often recall reading John F. Gilby's entertaining book *Secret Fighting Arts of The World*, in which he tells of his meeting with a famous *savate* (French kick-boxing) expert. In that account Gilby describes how this small man demonstrated his skill and incredible accuracy by repeatedly kicking the author's ear lobes with roundhouse kicks until they began to sting unbearably! The *savate* man made the point that he did not need to possess great strength or power in order to inflict pain. He simply had to strike, with the lightest of touch, a delicate target with breathtaking precision and speed.

The undeniable fact is that, provided competitors are adequately trained in the proper control of techniques, which is after all a characteristic of authentic karate, the safer option will always be that of no protective equipment other than the aforementioned gumshield, groin guard and breast protector.

5 REFEREES' TERMS AND SIGNALS

The following descriptions will enable you to familiarize yourself with all the terms and signals used in WSKA competition karate. These have been adopted by all the major *Shotokan* associations, including the KUGB. As a practising *karateka*, many of the Japanese terms will already be familiar to you, but you will undoubtedly find many others that are exclusive to the competition arena. You should study them carefully. In the next section it will be shown how they are applied during the course of a *kumite* match.

Rei

This is the referee's request for the competitors to bow to each other prior to, and after, fighting. The bow is symbolic in that it indicates respect and an acknowledgement that each is aware of the other's skill, and should therefore not be taken lightly. Implicit in this simple gesture, which should be performed correctly, is a code of conduct that dictates that victory will be secured, but not at any cost. It tells your opponent that you will endeavour to beat him using all your skills, but fairly and within a specified format that includes the use of agreed techniques. With your bow, you are projecting an air of dignity and are demonstrating an adherence to a ritualistic form of combat,

complete with rules and regulations, rather like a duel. Any subsequent actions or behaviour that violates this ritual will be interpreted as disrespectful and an ignorance of the significance of the bow. Bowing rituals are also undertaken prior to the first match commencing and at the end of the proceedings. These involve all participants, both officials and competitors. The referee instructs everyone to turn and bow to the dignitaries (the audience) with the words '*Shomen ni rei*'. He then motions for the competitors to turn and bow to the judges, '*Shimpan ni rei*', and finally for competitors to bow to their respective opponents, '*Octagai ni rei*'.

Yoi

Following the bow, the referee instructs the competitors to prepare for sparring by calling '*Yoi*' (ready). This is the cue for the fighters to 'switch on' both mentally and physically. Procuring a constant awareness or *zanshin* which must be maintained until the referee stops the bout is more difficult than the casual observer may imagine. Even a transient lack of concentration can cost an otherwise sharp competitor the contest, which underlines the need for absolute discipline and unwavering attention on the opponent.

FIGURE 1: The referee's start position.

FIGURE 2: *Tsuzukete hajime.*

Hajime

This is the referee's instruction to the competitors to begin or restart the match. When '*Hajime*' is called to begin the match, it is preceded by the announcement '*Shobu-ippon*', which means competition to one point, or '*Shobu-sanbon*', which means competition to three points. Elimination bouts are usually decided by *ippon* and the final itself by *sanbon*. The referee, having requested that the competitors mutually bow, then proclaims the match to be scored using either one or three points to determine victory – for example '*Shobu-ippon . . . hajime*'. Competitors must ensure that, at the referee's call and signal to begin, their concentration is absolute, so that, aside from being attentive to the referee's commands, the opponent is the sole consideration. For the duration of the match, all other considerations must be secondary. When restarting the match following a temporary stop, the referee will call out '*Tsuzukete hajime*'. This command is signalled visually by the referee and is illustrated in Figure 2.

Yame

This command is used by the referee to stop the fighters immediately. It is used in conjunction with the signal illustrated in Figure 3. Used on its own, the term 'Yame' indicates a temporary suspension of the match. If one or both fighters have moved outside the fighting area (jogai), the referee will proclaim 'Yame! Jogai nakae' to stop the match, and order the fighters back to their starting lines, 'Motonoichi'. If the time expires, or a competitor scores the required points to win the match, the referee calls out 'Yame! Soremade' to declare the end of the match.

There are several other conditions under which the referee will temporarily stop a match. These include instances when the referee notices a competitor committing or about to commit a prohibited act, when he asks a competitor to adjust his uniform, or when he deems that a match cannot continue due to illness or injury of one or both participants. The referee will also temporarily stop a match to respond to signals from any of the corner judges regarding any of the above matters.

Waza-ari

The referee, having temporarily suspended the match, will award a half-point (signalling an effective technique), by calling out 'Waza-ari' and indicating to the scorer by extending downwards to the side the arm nearest the successful

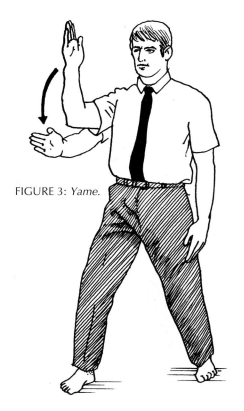

FIGURE 3: *Yame.*

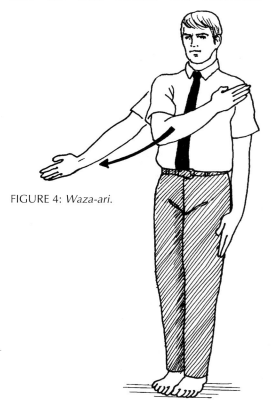

FIGURE 4: *Waza-ari.*

Ippon

Following 'Yame', this term declares that a full point, or decisive technique, has been scored, and if the match is held under *shobu-ippon* rules means the end of the match. As with the *waza-ari* signal, the arm nearest the successful competitor is used, but in this case it is extended higher than the shoulder. As previously, the referee may also state the title of the successful competitor and the winning technique.

Torimasen

This literally means 'no score', and can be used at the end of the allotted time to indicate that there has been no successful

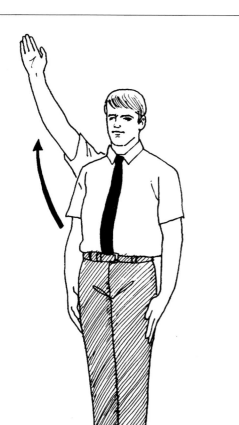

FIGURE 5: *Ippon.*

competitor. Fuller explanations of what fulfils the criteria for a successful *waza-ari* and the following *ippon* are given on pp. 43–45. It is commonplace for the referee also to state the title of the scorer and to specify the scoring technique; for example, '*Aka, chudan mawashi-geri, waza-ari*' – red competitor, middle level round-house kick, half-point. Under *shobu-ippon* rules, two half-points are needed in order to win a match. '*Awasete ippon*' means that two half-points have been scored and together represent one *ippon* (*awasewaza*).

FIGURE 6: *Torimasen.*

technique. Following this, the referee will call for a decision from the corner judges, based on other criteria as set down in the rules. Alternatively, the referee may order an extension to the match in order to determine a winner. This term and signal is used also following '*Aiuchi*', when it is considered that techniques were exchanged simultaneously thus cancelling each other out.

Aka (shiro) no katchi

The referee declares the winner (either red or white) using this term, simultaneously raising the corresponding arm as when awarding an *ippon*.

Hantei

Following the ending of the match, when there has been no decisive technique, the referee requests the opinion of the corner judges by uttering '*Hantei*' followed by a long whistle to instruct them to raise their flags. Once the result has been obtained, the referee gives a short whistle to request that they lower their flags.

Hikiwake

This may follow the above procedure and indicates a draw, where scores are even or the judges are unable to determine an outright winner. As well as stating '*Hikiwake*', the referee visually confirms this by signalling, using both arms as in Figure 7.

Encho

The referee makes this announcement to prolong the length of the match.

Aiuchi

Where two techniques are adjudged to have been delivered simultaneously, the

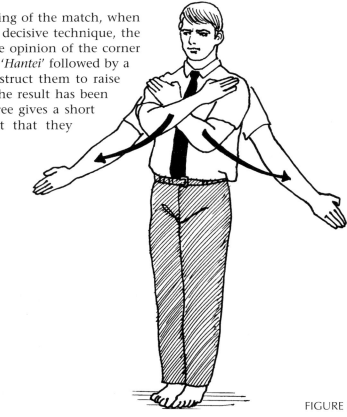

FIGURE 7: *Hikiwake*.

FIGURE 8: *Aiuchi*.

FIGURE 9: *Hansoku (make)*.

referee will utter '*Aiuchi*' and confirm this by touching both fists together in front of his chest as in Figure 8. This in effect means that it cannot be determined with any reliability which fighter's technique was most effective, and so no score is given. This signal is often followed by '*Torimasen*' and the corresponding signal.

Hansoku (make)

If a competitor commits a prohibited act (see Chapter 7) that is considered serious, particularly where the other competitor is deemed to be at risk, the referee will stop the fight and immediately announce a disqualification by sharply uttering '*Hansoku*' and indicating the offending competitor by extending the arm higher than the shoulder and pointing, as in Figure 9. Excessive contact, even where maliciousness is not suspected, is the most common reason for disqualification. In these circumstances it is usual for the referee then to award the match to the other competitor by stating '*Shiro (aka) hansoku, aka (shiro) no kachi*' – a foul by the white (red) competitor, therefore victory to the red (white) competitor.

Chui

This is a private warning, usually as a consequence of the referee noticing an act that infringes the rules, such as stepping outside the match area. In this particular instance, the referee may be heard to say to a competitor, '*Jogai*' (meaning area), which is a private warning that the offence has been committed. Only one private warning is given, so should the offence, or anything similar, be repeated, a public warning will be issued.

Hansoku chui

This indicates a foul or public warning and is given when an act is committed that is regarded as being serious enough to endanger the other competitor, should it continue, or another act that is in direct breach of the rules. Two *hansoku chui* are regarded as *hansoku*. The referee signals his decision by using a similar gesture as in *hansoku*, except that in this case the arm is extended well below the shoulder.

Shiro (aka) no kiken niyori aka (shiro) no kachi

The referee awards the match to the red (white) competitor because the white (red) competitor has withdrawn.

Atoshibaraku

A short bell or buzzer is sounded which indicates that there are only 30 seconds remaining of the match. The referee may state 'Atoshibaraku' as confirmation.

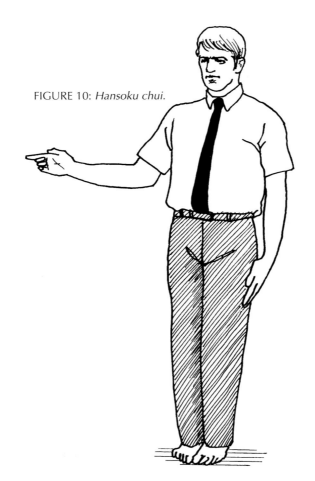

FIGURE 10: *Hansoku chui.*

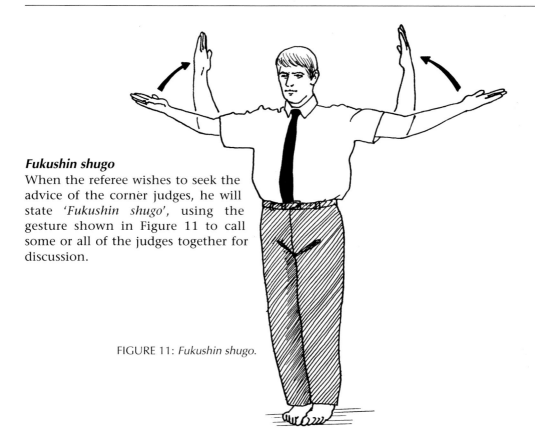

Fukushin shugo

When the referee wishes to seek the advice of the corner judges, he will state *'Fukushin shugo'*, using the gesture shown in Figure 11 to call some or all of the judges together for discussion.

FIGURE 11: *Fukushin shugo.*

Not proper distance

The referee indicates that a technique, although close, was delivered short of the target and does not merit a score.

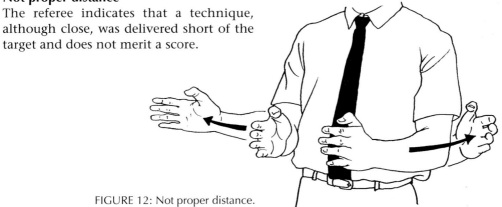

FIGURE 12: Not proper distance.

No (or weak) focus

This signal describes a technique that, despite striking the target, is considered to have been delivered with little or no power. Again, no score is awarded.

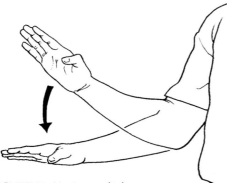

FIGURE 13: No (or weak) focus.

Blocked

The referee here indicates that an attack has been successfully blocked, or alternatively that it struck an arm instead of the target area.

FIGURE 14: Blocked.

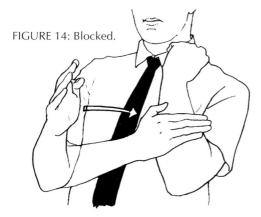

Out of target area

This signal indicates a technique that narrowly missed the target area, therefore no score is awarded.

FIGURE 15: Out of target area.

FIGURE 16: Out of time.

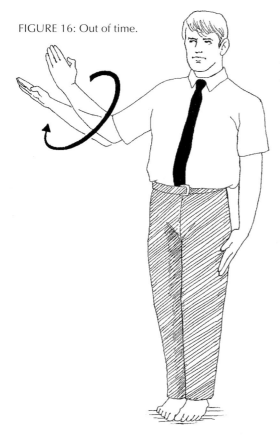

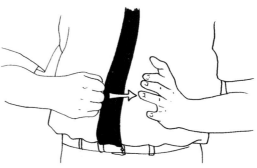

FIGURE 17: Contact.

Out of time

A gesture used by the referee to signal that a technique was delivered after '*Yame*' was called at the end of the allotted time, and therefore does not qualify for a score.

Contact

Here, the referee, by punching into his open palm, signals that excessive contact has been made by a competitor. This is usually followed by a public warning or even disqualification for the offending competitor.

6 JUDGES' SIGNALS

Listed below are the judges' signals, usually accompanied by a whistle to attract the referee's attention, to indicate the existence of a scoring technique or foul. Although the competitor should really only be concerned with the terms and signals as given by the referee, it is prudent also to be aware, wherever possible, of the meaning of the judges' signals.

Ready position

Figure 18 shows the corner judge's 'inactive' or ready position. He sits, fully attentive and focused on the action, ready to signal instantly by whistle and flag any score or foul by either competitor. His posture is erect and his forearms rest lightly on his thighs, holding a white flag in one hand and a red flag in the other.

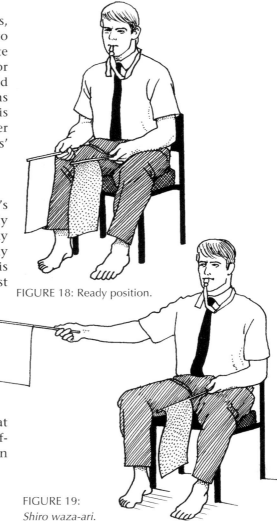

FIGURE 18: Ready position.

Shiro waza-ari

The judge has indicated his opinion that the white competitor has scored a half-point, and attracts the referee's attention by blowing his whistle.

FIGURE 19:
Shiro waza-ari.

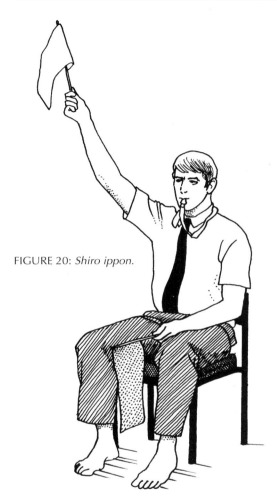

FIGURE 20: *Shiro ippon.*

discretion in requesting advice from those judges he feels were in the best position to form a reliable opinion. It could be, however, that at the critical moment the referee himself prevented the judge from seeing what actually happened, by unavoidably obstructing the judge's line of vision. It may also be that the judge was simply unable to see clearly owing to the competitors themselves being in a less than ideal position. It is a requirement that all referees and judges act impartially and are unbiased, and therefore they can only comment on what they actually see. If there is the slightest doubt, then an opinion is not given and *mienai* is signalled. The judge does not, in this situation, blow his whistle.

Shiro ippon
The judge indicates the existence of an *ippon*, delivered by the white competitor, and indicates this by blowing his whistle and sharply raising his white flag.

Mienai
The judge usually makes this gesture when unsighted if the referee looks to him for clarification. The referee uses his

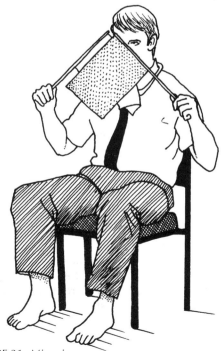

FIGURE 21: *Mienai.*

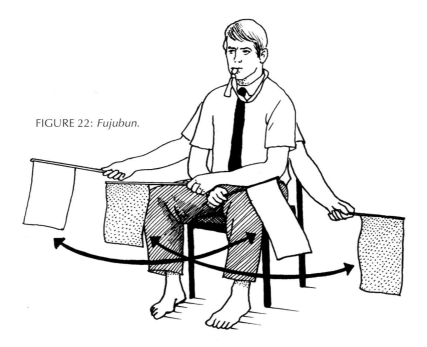

FIGURE 22: *Fujubun.*

Fujubun

Like the referee's signal *torimasen*, the crossing of the flags, followed by both being extended to either side, indicates the judge's opinion that a scoring technique was not delivered to a target. The judge may repeat this action several times. There is no whistle.

Aiuchi

Just as the referee declares that there has been a simultaneous exchange of techniques by poking his fists together, the judge indicates the same by poking the ends of each flag to each other. Again there is no whistle.

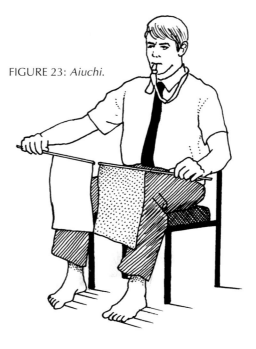

FIGURE 23: *Aiuchi.*

Jogai

Here the judge blows his whistle sharply and intermittently to draw the attention of the referee to the fact that, in this case, the white competitor has stepped outside the contest area.

Hansoku chui

By blowing his whistle and moving the white flag overhead in small circles, the judge indicates that the white competitor has committed a foul.

Hansoku (make)

By waving the white flag in large circular motion above his head, the judge declares

FIGURE 24: *Jogai.*

FIGURE 25: *Hansoku chui.*

FIGURE 26: *Hansoku (make).*

that the white competitor has committed an act that warrants disqualification.

Hikiwake

Crossing both flags above his head, the judge makes this signal on the referee's request for decision to indicate that, in his opinion, the match is a draw.

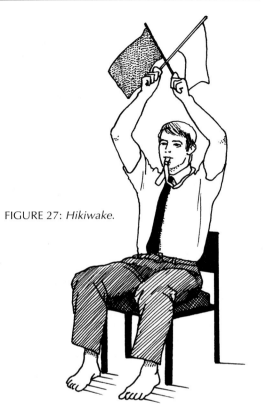

FIGURE 27: *Hikiwake.*

7 PROHIBITED ACTS AND BEHAVIOUR

Most well-trained *karateka* are highly disciplined and are capable of considerable self-control, even under stressful conditions. It is, however, a sad fact that there are still individuals who readily forget the *dojo* code and think only of winning. This kind of attitude has a profound effect on behaviour and invariably leads to a conflict with the rules and ethics of both competition and karate as an art. An uninformed reader, seeing the following list, could be forgiven for thinking that martial artists in general are bloodthirsty psychopaths. The truth, thankfully, is that competitions organized by official bodies, conducted by properly trained judges with highly skilled exponents, are very disciplined and orderly, with very little evidence of the disgraceful behaviour we see exhibited in many other sports.

Nevertheless, the rules of any game must take into account acts or behaviour that by their nature compromise the aims of the sport, and punish offenders accordingly. Karate is no exception, and, perhaps because we are dealing with a fighting art, it is for some individuals all too easy to cross the line that divides sport from fighting art. As *karateka* are required to attack each other with a display of what might under any other circumstances be considered outright aggression, it is perhaps little wonder that the following rules have been instigated!

Acts or behaviour that will result in disqualification are as follows.

- Failing to obey the instructions of the referee.

- Becoming over-excited, or reckless, to such a degree that a competitor is considered to be a danger to his opponent.

- Any acts or behaviour considered by the referee to be malicious, dangerous or in direct violation of the rules.

- Continual escapes out of the match area (*jogai*). After the first escape, the referee will give a private warning. After the second escape, a public or official warning is given, '*Jogai chui*'. Should a competitor escape for a third time, he may be disqualified, '*Jogai hansoku*'.

- Any unruly behaviour or act by supporters or manager, or anyone connected with a competitor, which offends the etiquette of the *dojo*; this may result in the disqualification of the team or individual.

- Any other behaviour that violates the rules of the match.

In addition, the rules of the *kumite* match dictate that all the acts and techniques listed below are prohibited. Any competitor failing to observe these rules will be given a private warning, an official warning or even be disqualified. These rules ensure proper conduct and the safety of the opponents.

- Attacking an opponent in an uncontrolled manner.

- Using open-hand attacking techniques, such as *shuto-uchi* (knife-hand strike).

- Direct attacks to the groin.

- Attacking any joints, or the insteps.

- Grabbing, wrestling or bodily crashing against an opponent unnecessarily.

- Using throwing techniques that could put an opponent in jeopardy.

- Making deliberate repeated escapes out of the match area, or any moves which are considered to waste time.

- Behaving in an unsporting manner by swearing, using provocation or any other behaviour which is regarded as being offensive.

- Behaving in any manner which brings karate into disrepute.

8 HOW TO WIN

The rules state that victory is awarded on the basis of scoring an *ippon*, which may be two *waza-ari*, victory by the judges' *hantei*, or defeat as a result of *hansoku chui*, *hansoku make* or *kiken niyori*.

The designated scoring areas are the head and neck, the chest, abdomen and back. Attacks to any other area are either illegal or will not be recognized.

SCORING AN *IPPON* – THE CRITERIA

In order to score a full point the *karateka* will need to use a controlled, authorized technique and deliver it with exactness to a recognized target area with decisiveness and focused power, or *kime*. In addition, it is required that the strike be delivered while the *karateka* is exhibiting good form, the correct martial attitude, spirit, proper timing and correct distancing. To elaborate on this, a technique may fail to qualify as an *ippon* even if it is delivered with proper timing to the correct target. If it is not backed up with the correct attitude and fighting spirit, it will not be considered to be a decisive technique. Just because a kick connects – even to *jodan* (the head area), a full point will not necessarily be awarded, unless it is delivered with fighting spirit. Conversely, a competitor who displays good fighting spirit but poor technique is also unlikely to score. This is where the development of good basics is so important, as all aspects of karate are emphasized equally. The *karateka* need only then apply all those aspects with equal commitment to do well in *kumite*.

Observation often reveals that many competitors, while displaying good form, fail to project fighting spirit. It should be recognized that the *kiai* (spirit shout) is an indispensable method of externalizing the spirit and therefore should be developed to become as natural as blocking, kicking and punching.

Competitors who may have good form and yet fail to display their spirit in this way wonder why full points are not awarded. To guarantee a full point where a score is effected, you should deliver your techniques with an attitude of 'all or nothing' – anything less and you (never mind the referee) should consider it undeserving of *ippon*.

Situations that merit an *ippon* are as follows.

- When an opponent prepares to move forward, he is nullified by a perfectly timed scoring technique.

- When an opponent is foot-swept or

thrown off balance and a scoring technique is delivered instantly.

- When a combination of successive and effective scoring techniques overwhelm the opponent so that he is unable to defend himself. This may be, for example, a combined use of effective *tsuki* and *keri* techniques, or a combined use of effective *tsuki* and *nage* (throwing) techniques.

- When the opponent, having lost his fighting spirit, turns away from his attacker so that he is struck from behind.

- Any effective scoring technique delivered to undefended target areas of the opponent's body.

Instances where *ippon* shall not be scored, even if delivered with sufficient power, are as follows.

- When a competitor hesitates; for example, having seized the initiative he fails to take advantage of the opportunity to score immediately.

- When, having foot-swept his opponent, a competitor fails to deliver a scoring technique immediately.

- When a technique is delivered outside the match area. However, an *ippon* may be awarded if it is considered that the competitor delivering the technique was inside the boundary of the match area at the time he delivered the technique.

- Any scoring technique will be rendered invalid if it is delivered after the referee's call of 'Yame'.

A scoring technique that fulfils most of the criteria of *ippon*, but is lacking in some respect, will be awarded a half-point or *waza-ari*. The distinction between a full point and a half-point is best defined by considering *ippon* to be a 'decisive' scoring technique, whereas a *waza-ari* is regarded to be an 'effective' scoring technique.

THE CRITERIA FOR DECISION IN THE ABSENCE OF *IPPON*

Should the time of the match expire with no clear winner, in the absence of *ippon* or defeat owing to a foul or disqualification, the panel of judges will be required to indicate their preference based on certain criteria. The referee, having called 'Yame', orders the fighters back to their respective starting lines, and, having given the judges time to consider their verdict, calls 'Hantei'. By blowing his whistle, he signals to the judges to indicate their opinion by raising their flags, and then awards the match by majority decision. A fighter who scores a single *waza-ari* would be declared the victor under these circumstances. In the absence of any score, however, other criteria are taken into account. These include whether there has been any infringement of the rules for which a fighter has been warned, and the comparative skill, fighting attitude, strategy and number of attacking moves demonstrated. In addition, where there is no clear winner, the judges may declare

OPPOSITE World Shotokan Karate Association (WSKA) Championship 1995. This female *karateka* utters a powerful *kiai* during her performance in the individual *kata* event.

the competitor who demonstrated the greatest vigour and best fighting spirit to be the victor. In the event of a tie, the referee has the authority to decide victory by his casting vote.

Throughout the duration of the match, the corner judges signal to the referee by using their whistles and flags, where they consider that a scoring technique has been delivered, or a foul has been committed. The referee can overrule the signal of a single judge, but where two or more judges make the same signal he will stop the match temporarily, and call 'Fukushin shugo' to summon the judges concerned in order to make a decision.

Where the two-referee, or 'mirror', system is in operation, one is designated as the chief referee and conducts the match, while the other acts in the capacity of assistant referee. He indicates his opinion to the chief referee continually through the use of the agreed signals, and may be called upon to give verbal advice.

INJURIES AND ACCIDENTS DURING THE MATCH

Where it is considered that a competitor who is unable to continue was injured as a result of an accident, he is declared the loser. Should both competitors suffer accidental injury, perhaps as a result of a clash which prevents either from continuing, the referee declares the match a draw, 'Hikiwake'. Any decision made as a consequence of injury is reached following consultation with the championship doctor. A competitor may withdraw from a match of his own volition for a variety of reasons, including a loss of fighting spirit, nerves or some other physiological reason. In this case, the referee declares him the loser.

PROTESTS

It is forbidden for any team member personally to make a protest against the judges' decision. Where it is suspected that the decision by the referee and judges is in obvious violation of the rules, the competitor's team manager may complain to the arbitrator who gives his personal attention to the matter and, following consultation with the judges, makes a decision. In the rare case where a complaint is upheld, the arbitrator has the power to demand that the judges revise their decision.

9 KUMITE EVENTS

THE INDIVIDUAL EVENT

The duration of a match is normally two minutes, although extensions can be ordered by the referee to determine a victor. Where extensions are ordered it is usually for an extra one minute. In the case where a match is carried over to three rounds, the referee announces a winner based on a majority decision. The time starts for each match when the referee calls 'Hajime', but is temporarily suspended should the referee wish to consult with the judges or attend to a competitor who has been injured. With the referee's call 'Tsuzukete hajime' the clock is restarted. A time-keeper is appointed in all *kumite* events; his responsibility is to time the duration of a match accurately, taking into consideration any temporary suspensions.

As previously stated, elimination matches are usually conducted using the 'mirror' judging system. With only two pairs of eyes focused on the action, it is perhaps inevitable that errors in judgement may occur more frequently than will be expected when five judges are in attendance, as with the flag system. Having said that, with the mirror system the close proximity to the action of both referees may enable them to judge better the effectiveness of any technique.

Certainly, there are advantages to using the mirror system for the elimination rounds in any championship. A big plus is that referees and judges, who are always in short supply, can be utilized more efficiently to whittle down the entries quickly to a more manageable quota. Using this method, each 'pool' of competitors, and there may be as many as 50 to each pool, can be 'dealt with' using just two judges – one being the chief referee and the other his assistant.

As with any event, the referee has sole control over the individual match and, as in the case of the flag system where a judge indicates a scoring technique or a foul by signalling, the referee may choose to ignore a signal made by his assistant. In doing this, he overrules the advice of the assistant referee, but more often than not the chief referee will call a temporary stop in order to obtain the advice of his assistant. Elimination bouts are usually fought to a single *ippon* or *awasewaza* (two half-points constituting a full point), which in turn makes for shorter bouts. The finals are usually longer affairs, being the best of three *ippons*, and judged by the flag system (Figure 28).

THE TEAM EVENT

Again, it is usual for elimination bouts to be conducted, for convenience, using the

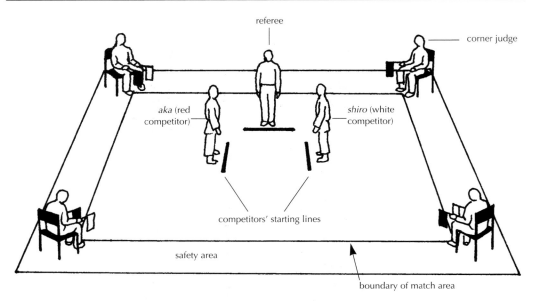

referee

corner judge

aka (red competitor)

shiro (white competitor)

competitors' starting lines

safety area

boundary of match area

FIGURE 28: The match area set up for the individual/team *kumite* event, using the flag system.

mirror system. In this case, most of the above rules apply. The fighting order is decided by the team captain who submits this list to the desk prior to the event. No changes can be made to this order thereafter. The winning team is decided on the basis of the number of winners of individual matches. Each match is normally decided on the basis of one *ippon*. Where there is a draw, the number of *ippons* scored is taken into account, so that the team scoring the majority of full points is declared the winner. Included in this is the number of *awasewaza ippons*, or two half-point victories amounting to a full point, scored in any of the matches. Should the number of *awasewaza ippons* be equal, then the team scoring the most full *ippons* is declared the winner. Matches that are won as the result of a foul, disqualification or voluntary retirement of the opponent are counted as a full *ippon*. In the event that teams tie, even after

applying all the methods of decision above, the referee orders that one representative from each team fight each other in order to determine the winner. If the match fails to produce a winner after two extensions, further representatives will be put forward from each team, their names having been given before the first extra match takes place.

THE *IPPON KUMITE* EVENT

This is a new, and at present children-only, event. It bridges the gap between *kata* and *kumite* admirably, in that it requires the kind of precision and attention to technical detail that one may ordinarily associate with the performance of *kata*. However, as the drill requires the use of a partner, other skills vital in *kumite*, such as appropriate distancing, accuracy, timing and sharp reflexes are necessary. So the *ippon kumite*

The two-man or 'mirror' system of refereeing in action at the 1997 KUGB Nationals. Facing is A. (Ron) Hicks, a fine *karateka* who, like many qualified referees, has himself competed successfully.

event can be regarded as a marriage of both categories, with the successful competitor exhibiting the qualities common in both disciplines in addition to those that are exclusive to one or the other. Competitors should remember that they are performing a basic sparring routine, so that there should be no 'bouncing' around or baulking, as one would do to obtain an advantage in *jyu kumite*.

In common with other *kumite* events, competitors are identified as *aka* and *shiro*. There are the usual bowing formalities, and then both take it in turns to attack and defend, with the requirement that the attacker states clearly the techniques and the target. Only the attacks are pre-arranged, so that the defender is able to exercise freedom of choice in countering. Just as with the elimination rounds of the individual *kata*, the competitors are judged using the flag system.

10 KATA EVENTS

THE INDIVIDUAL EVENT

Following the formal bowing ceremony at the start of the eliminations, which is conducted by the chief referee, all competitors are instructed to be seated at the edge of the area. The judges take up their seated positions at the corners of the area and hold their flags in the ready position as shown in Figure 29. The announcer calls out the names of the first two competitors, who are designated *shiro* and *aka*, with the latter donning a red belt for identification purposes. Both competitors approach the edge of the match area and await the referee's signal to approach the starting lines. With his signal, they both bow and enter the area, taking up their positions on the starting lines facing the referee. After consulting his list, the referee announces the prescribed *kata*.

The prescribed *kata* for KUGB elimination rounds are usually the five *heian kata*. The only restrictions imposed here are determined by the *kyu* level of the competitors. The referee will not expect a competitor to perform a *kata* which is above the *karateka*'s level as indicated by the colour of his belt; for example, a yellow belt (7th *kyu*) would not be asked to perform *heian godan*.

Having stated the required *kata* to be performed, the referee sometimes also confirms his choice by indicating the *kata* number with his fingers. This can be helpful for the competitors, particularly in a noisy arena, where the frequent sound of spirited *kiai* can be distracting. Hence, the referee may call '*Heian yondan*' and indicate this by raising his hand and showing four fingers. On the completion of the *kata*, the referee will instruct '*Yame*' to order the contestants to return to natural stance. After a pause of approximately 10 seconds to enable the other judges to make their decision, he blows his whistle to call upon the judges to announce their choice. After evaluating the judges' decisions, the referee again blows his whistle and raises the appropriate flag to announce the winner.

In the circumstance where a competitor fails to complete his *kata* and his opponent completes his without error, the latter will be declared the winner. The referee can make this decision without consulting the judges.

The signals used by the judges are identical to those used in the *kumite* event, although there are far fewer of them. The judges announce the victor by raising either the red or the white flag in the same way as is indicated in the *kumite* for the award of an *ippon*. Again, to indicate *hikiwake*, a draw, the flags are crossed above the head. To obtain the opinion of the judges in the case where an

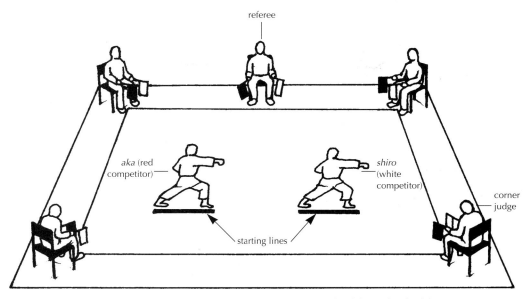

FIGURE 29: The match area set up for the elimination rounds of the individual *kata* event, using the flag system.

error in performance is suspected, the referee also uses the recognized signal, as shown in Figure 11.

There unfortunately exists a great deal of subjectivity when it comes to deciding what constitutes the performance of a good *kata*. It seems that, even given the criteria, some judges appear to hold steadfastly onto their own views on what makes one performance better than another. Where one competitor is obviously more skilful than another, there is little problem. The difficulties arise, however, when all the necessary qualities that define a good *kata* are displayed by both competitors. The judges then may rely on more abstract criteria, such as style, or personal preference regarding the way a particular sequence in a *kata* is performed. There have been, quite frankly, ridiculous suggestions that a competitor should be penalized for exhaling too noisily, or failing to finish on an exact spot. Such arguments would seem to indicate that some judges are unable to apply the prescribed criteria and choose instead to base their decisions on what really amounts to pseudo-technical trivia.

Regardless of this, for *kata* the following criteria should form the basis for judgement.

- The *kata* sequence. All techniques and stances should follow the prescribed form with no deviation.

- The quality of the technique. This includes the control of power, externalized by *kime* or focus. Related to this is tension and contraction in the correct manner, speed and the control of rhythm. Breathing should be properly controlled and harmonious with the technique.

51

- Direction of movement. This simply means that it is not enough to perform the correct stances and techniques; one must also follow the correct *embusen* or performance line.

- The contestant should throughout his performance exhibit an understanding of the purpose of the techniques he is performing.

- There should be visible awareness of what the *karateka* sees in his mind's eye, best exemplified by eye intensity. The eyes should not wander aimlessly or be distracted, but should be focused intently on the imagined opponent.

- Each technique should be equally strong so that none is superfluous. Some *karateka* give the impression that they favour certain techniques at the expense of others. A competitor of poor quality will reveal this by performing certain parts of a *kata* with vigour, only to fade with those sequences, or components, that he finds difficult.

- Perhaps one of the most important aspects of performing a *kata* is spirit. It is relatively easy to display spirit in a *kumite* match, as one has a live, breathing opponent to contend with. Many competitors find it difficult to 'switch on' for the performance of a *kata*, presuming it to be relatively unimportant. For those individuals, it is 'correctness' that concerns them, evidenced by their careful performance in case they should falter, and yet it is fighting spirit that must be the dominant factor.

- The performer must convey a strong attitude, and an indomitable spirit. The performance should be proud with the attitude unwavering and filled with dignity.

In addition to the above points, judges are expected to be able to evaluate a *kata* not simply on the basis of whether it is good or bad, but whether it accords with the essential elements of each basis for judgement. Judges are furthermore reminded that, because they are assessing a performance within the constraints of a competition, they must take into account the slightest error. This brings us back to the difficult territory of what constitutes an error. A major mistake, such as the omission of a technique, an incorrect stance or sequence, is easily spotted. Observation needs to be particularly keen, however, when a competitor, for example, strikes with *tettsui-uchi* instead of *uraken-uchi*. Unless one is looking in anticipation for such a mistake, the speed of the technique, plus having at the same time to evaluate form generally, will make it very difficult to spot such an error.

Coupled with this, during the eliminations, the judges have to switch concentration very rapidly from one competitor to the other. This makes it very difficult to make a direct comparison, especially where the competitors are moving at exactly the same speed. It is often simpler to compare performances when they are slightly out of synchronization, so that the competitor slightly ahead in time can be first observed performing a

OPPOSITE KUGB National Championship 1997. The dynamic Sean Roberts midway through his winning performance of *niju-shiho*. Despite suffering from jet-lag, having just returned from Hawaii, he successfully defended his title for the fifth year in succession.

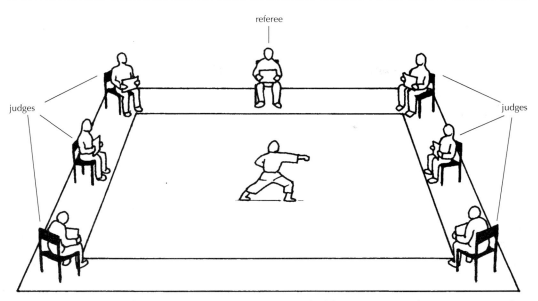

referee

judges

judges

FIGURE 30: The match area set up for the finals of the individual *kata* event, using the points system. This system is also used for the team *kata* event.

particular sequence, before switching attention to the one slightly behind. In this way, a fairly accurate assessment of the relative skills of the performers is possible.

The points system (Figure 30) used for the finals is arguably a better method of judgement. Unlike the flag system, here the judges, of which there are seven including the chief referee, are able to apply a score to each individual perform-ance they witness, each competitor per-forming by himself. Raising a flag can only permit a judge to give a clear winner, with no indication on just how close a judgement may be, unless both flags are crossed and raised above the head to indicate a draw. The points system is a far more interesting method of judgement, as it allows the judges the freedom to express their opinion by rating a performance on a scale. Each judge carries a scoreboard which is split down the centre. There are two sets of cards numbered from 0 to 9, one set black and one red; the black numbers are used to represent whole numbers and the red ones to represent tenths. Before the competition the chief judge determines the average score, for example 7.0. The judges can then, upon viewing each *kata*, decide whether a performance merits a higher or lower than average score. Out of the seven scores received, the highest and lowest scores are disregarded, with the remaining five being added together to produce a final score.

Should two competitors tie on points,

OPPOSITE Welsh international Jane George shows good concentration, correct posture and eye intensity as she executes a powerful interpretation of *kanku-dai*.

Team *kata*. Synchronization is vital, but judges will also be looking at individual performances within the team.

both are asked to repeat the performance, or at their own discretion may choose a different *kata*. The procedure in the finals is somewhat different in that a *karateka*, once called to the area, and having bowed, is allowed to begin and end his *kata* without the instruction of the referee. One by one, all finalists will perform their chosen *kata* in this way, bowing on leaving the match area after receiving their respective scores from the announcer.

THE TEAM EVENT

Team *kata* is usually judged using the points system, as opposed to the faster flag system. This is because it would simply be asking too much of the judges to evaluate the performance of six contestants, all moving simultaneously! The number of entrants in this category remains, not surprisingly, well below that of other events, given that the training for this event requires three *karateka* to train exclusively together in order to perfect their timing. The way in which regular *dojo* sessions are conducted can sometimes make it difficult to facilitate this kind of special training, which means that individuals comprising a team often have to train outside of *dojo* time.

In keeping with the finals of the individual event, there is no need to separate teams by identifying one as *aka* and the other as *shiro*, as teams do not compete at the same time. The announcer calls a team to the match area by their *dojo* name and, having bowed, the three members walk in formation into the area and bow again to the chief referee on reaching their starting lines. The three members form the points of an equilateral triangle if viewed from above; they are equidistant from each other. There is no exact official measurement for this distance; suffice it to say that it should be sufficient to permit freedom of movement for each individual and great enough to allow the judges to see all of the members simultaneously.

The leader of the team, who always stands at the forward point of the triangle, calls '*Rei*', so that all bow in unison, announces the chosen *kata* and then instructs '*Yoi*', followed by '*Hajime*'. On the completion of the *kata*, the leader then calls '*Yame*' and '*Rei*'.

As a demonstration event, team *kata* is gaining in popularity. Nowadays, team *kata* can comprise all male members, all female or a combination. It is the only category that enables male and female *karateka* to compete together, and demands the utmost in precision timing. The slightest error in this respect on the part of one individual can destroy the coherence of the group, so training is geared towards developing an almost instinctive awareness of the other members of the team.

11 ATTITUDE, ETIQUETTE AND CONVENTION

With the development of sport karate, there is evidence that in some respects there has been an erosion of what has always been considered the most important aspects of *karate-do*. Master Gichin Funakoshi, the father of modern karate, placed greatest emphasis on the study of karate – not on the physical skills, as might be expected, but on the moulding and development of a strong moral character. We only have to examine a typical karate class to realize that most students train in a very superficial way. Whereas they may pay some cursory homage to the inherent code of behaviour and the philosophical principles, in many instances it soon becomes obvious that training is undertaken simply as a way of keeping fit, for self-defence, or to win competitions.

It is an unfortunate fact that most students do not continue to train through-out their lives. Once the coveted black belt has been gained, or the championship has been won, interest and commitment fades rapidly, to be replaced by what are perceived to be more rewarding pursuits. This is evidenced by the vast numbers of students who pass regularly through the *dojo*, pausing long enough only to collect a few belts or trophies. Sport karate can encourage this attitude. Every *sensei* or teacher occasionally comes across a 'natural' – a student who is instinctively able to apply and develop skills in a very short space of time. The danger here is that such a student may be encouraged to train only in superficial strategies and clever tricks, designed to out-time skilful opponents, for the express purpose of claiming a prize. They may be coached in *kata* to 'look' good, and may actually become a *kata* champion, without ever attaining any real knowledge about the deeper meaning of their performance.

This all sounds very cynical, but I make no apologies. I have seen far too many promising students come into karate who, having been seduced by the glamour and prestige of winning competitions, do so at the expense of honest, committed training. For any real benefits to be gained from training, the only objective that will deliver lasting satisfaction is a lifelong commit-ment, a journey in pursuit not only of physical perfection but also of self-en-lightenment. It is unimportant that perfec-tion may be impossible to attain, as it is the journey along which the student travels that reveals the true values. Those *karateka* who have trained for many years will agree that the longer that journey is, the greater are the rewards. To put it another way;

karate is not only a sport, a means of self-defence, or a mere physical exercise. True, it is all of these things, and yet it is much, much more. The sporting aspect of karate is just that, an aspect – a facet of a many-sided jewel.

I believe that the responsibility for guiding a student down the right road rests firmly on the shoulders of the *sensei* or instructor. If all that interests an instructor is gaining recognition and prestige through his student, then that is cause for regret. Right from the very beginning, all students should be encouraged to train correctly with the right attitude, equally on all aspects of *karate-do*, even though they may, for example, have a natural propensity for *kumite*. Of course strengths should be encouraged, but that is not to say that weaknesses should be neglected. In fact, the perseverance and dedication to overcome these very weaknesses are the kind of attributes that lead to the development of the qualities that typify the true *karateka*. We all feel most comfortable doing the things that require little or no effort. Anything else is an exertion and true to human nature, given a choice, we invariably take the easiest option. The study of *karate-do* consistently requires the student to confront adversity head-on.

By confronting obstacles and overcoming them through application, sheer determination, and persistence, the character is given a thorough 'workout', just as, in a physical sense, commitment to a weight-training schedule will produce results. This process has a habit of permeating all facets of an individual's life. The value of training sincerely in this way can therefore be seen to have a positive effect on the way in which a person feels about himself and consequently how he relates to the wider world. Once these important issues are acknowledged, even if not fully appreciated, then a competitor can enjoy, with a clear conscience, the challenge of testing his skills against another for the benefit of an audience.

Training for competition should be no different. It should be undertaken with the correct attitude and recognized for what it is, a facet of *karate-do*. It is the facet that generally appeals to the young, who are more inclined to want to test themselves against their peers. As the years advance, however, most students lose not only the speed and athleticism required in modern competition but also the ambition. To the true *karateka*, young or old, the arena is simply an extension of the *dojo*, not something particularly special and certainly not the epitome of karate training. If all that one desires from karate are trophies, then that would indicate a very shallow understanding of *karate-do*. So all young *karateka* would do well to recognize that entering competitions is a temporary part of karate, and that, should they wish to continue practising karate, they will one day have to pursue other, less obvious rewards.

All practising *karateka* would do well to study and apply the following *dojo-kun* (code) to appreciate the depth and true philosophy of *karate-do*.

- Exert oneself in the perfection of character.

- Be faithful and sincere.

- Cultivate the spirit of perseverance.

- Respect propriety.

- Refrain from impetuous and violent behaviour.

This simple and yet profound code must be applied by all competitors. Behaviour and attitude should be of the highest order. Proper conduct and etiquette, if adhered to at all times, not only ensure that karate is portrayed in the best possible light to the general public but also guarantee the safety of fellow competitors. Over-excitement, recklessness or an inattention to the rules all add up to unacceptable risks. It is every *karateka*'s responsibility to make sure that he enters competition with a good appreciation of the rules, having properly prepared himself, both physically and mentally. Anyone who enters otherwise does so without regard for the proper spirit of *karate-do*.

It is worthwhile underlining the importance of behaving in a sportsmanlike manner. If you have already competed, you will appreciate that it is inevitable that poor decisions will sometimes be made. Accepting that the judges are skilled and unbiased, there will always be human error. The wise competitor will acknowledge this, realizing that there will be occasions when poor decisions will actually be cast in his favour. Accepting defeat graciously, even with the knowledge of an unfair decision, is testament to the maturity of the competitor and a display of good sportsmanship. We see, in many sports, far too many examples of bad sportsmanship, where decisions are challenged by players in a very aggressive and undignified manner. Witnessing those very same players predictably failing to make as much noise when they are seen to benefit from a poor decision is a clear indication that, for those individuals, victory is the goal at any cost.

I hope that this book clarifies many of the often confusing rules that are an inevitability of something as complicated as a martial art such as karate. Perhaps it also provides a forum for healthy debate. If it prompts both competitors and officials to examine the rules in more detail then I shall consider it a success. Finally, if it inspires you to want to compete then I wish you the best of luck.

INDEX